Table of Contents

Introduction

What is Detox

Cleanse vs. Detox

The Whole Body Cleanse

Detox Diet

Detox Smoothie Recipes

Plant Based Diet

INTRODUCTION

Tired of obsessing about food all day? Have been tried multiple diets and failed?

If so, "Lose Up To 2 Pounds a Day by Drinking Smoothies: Delicious Detox Diet Recipes" might be for you!

In this book, you will learn:

What is the best detox drink to lose weight?

Can you lose weight by drinking smoothies?

What is the most effective plant based diet?

How much weight can you lose in a 3 day detox?

You will enjoy drinking smoothies made up of supernutrients from fruits and leafy greens.

Your body will be grateful for drinking smoothies as your energy and health improve to levels you never thought possible.

WHAT IS DETOX

I have a burning desire to explain the difference between the very fashionable craze that is known as "detoxing" and the process of actual detoxification. Knowing a bit about the workings of the body will help you understand the reason for doing a "detox" and choosing a plan that will actually help.

Detoxification is what our bodies do naturally, without any particular diet or particular plan – all day, every day, our body works and interacts with other organs to neutralise, transform and remove harmful substances (toxins).

Harmful substances are not just booze and ciggies, by the way!

Cheerfully, they are everywhere, unavoidable and a normal part of life; metabolite end products, pollution, pesticides on and in your food, pollutants found in water, stress, pharmaceutical drugs… the list is endless and the body works away the whole time removing them from our system.

Our livers filter 1.4 litres of blood every minute – that's every minute!

Filtering the blood requires two phases of detoxification. Phase one helps to neutralise baddies - this phase is where you need antioxidants such as glutathione and vitamins E and C.

Phase two adds chemicals to make the bad stuff soluble and possible for the body to excrete it.

This is where you need things like glutamine, glycine and sulphur foods such as cabbages and broccoli. Garlic is helpful for this stage too.

So does detoxing really work? And why do we all say we are "detoxing" when our bodies are detoxifying all the time anyway?

Your liver and your kidneys will take very good care of you come thick or thin, but the toxic load we carry is getting greater all the time.

There are many more pollutants these days, self-inflicted and unavoidable, so our organs of detoxification will be working harder than ever.

Detox plans usually consist of radically changing the way we normally eat, drink and behave; changing the food you eat to fresh, anti-inflammatory foods, increased plants, hydration and avoiding the toxic vices we may have.

Give Your Body Extra to Work

So, when people have a pop at the "detoxing" gang in January, or anytime, I think they might be the ones who are missing the trick.

By taking in a diet that is vastly superior on the nutrient front than your usual, you are bathing yourself with all sorts of helpful micronutrients that your liver needs for phase one and phase two of the process.

By changing our food, giving the wine and coffee a break, consuming supplements, and drinking drinks that are rich in the vitamins and minerals that our body uses in the liver pathways we SUPPORT our body in its daily battle with the baddies!

Giving your body a bit extra to work with, while reducing the stuff that slows our systems down from time to time makes total sense to me.

I often use protocols like the one below in my clinic with huge success.

Why?

Doing a "detox" plan can help your energy levels, your skin glow, your mood, your sleep, your weight, your sugar cravings (well why wouldn't it?

You are taking a little bit of self-care). It is good to try and reset once in a while.

This was part of the reason that I crated my five-day "detox" plan.

A delivered-to-your-home service that is based on eating super anti-inflammatory, high-fibre foods for four days and resting the gut by drinking only liquids for one day.

The results are amazing, plus my hope is that it inspires a better understanding of what food you can eat and feeling bloody great on.

Of course, there are many different ways to do a liver support plan. Protocols I would recommend would be a liquid fast for a maximum of three days, doing a juice, smoothie, soup, juice, soup pattern (and not Heinz tomato soup!).

I'm also a fan of vegan and plant-based meals as they offer a nice rest for the body by including nuts and seeds and avocados, for protein and happy fats.

Although detox is primarily thought of as a treatment for alcohol or drug dependence, the term is also used to refer to a short-term diet that proponents claim can facilitate toxin removal and promote weight loss.

Although there are many different types of detox diets, they generally follow the same principles:

Minimize the amount of chemicals ingested (for example, by eating organic food).

Emphasize foods that provide the vitamins, nutrients, and antioxidants that the body needs for detoxification.

Emphasize foods, such as fiber-rich foods and water, that increase the frequency of bowel movements and urination.

What you can eat and can't depends on the particular detox diet. Some involve juicing or drinking liquids. Others allow some foods, such as fruits and vegetables, or include a broader range of foods.

Some research suggests that many of the chemicals we ingest daily through food, water, and air can become deposited in fat cells in our bodies.

Toxins include pesticides, antibiotics and hormones in food, chemicals from food packaging, household cleaners, detergents, food additives, heavy metals, pollution, drugs, and cigarette smoke.

Proponents claim that the cumulative load, called the "body burden", may lead to illness and has been linked to hormonal imbalance, impaired immune function, and nutritional deficiencies.

Signs are said to include indigestion, poor concentration, tiredness, headaches, bad breath, poor skin, and muscle pain.

The basic idea behind detox diets is to temporarily give up certain kinds of foods that are thought to contain toxins.

The idea is to purify and purge the body of all the "bad" stuff. But the truth is, the human body is designed to purify itself.

Detox diets vary. Most involve some version of a fast: that is, giving up food for a couple of days and then gradually reintroducing certain foods into the diet. Many of these diets also encourage people to have colonic irrigation or enemas to "clean out" the colon. (An enema flushes out the rectum and colon using water.)

Others recommend that you take special teas or supplements to help the "purification" process.

There are lots of claims about what a detox diet can do, from preventing and curing disease to giving people more energy or focus.

Of course, eating a diet lower in fat and added sugars and higher in fiber can help many people feel healthier. But people who support detox diets claim that this is because of the elimination of toxins.

There's no scientific proof that these diets help rid the body of toxins faster or that the elimination of toxins will make you a healthier, more energetic person.

"Detox" used to mean many things, which may be part of the reason for the discrepancy.

To some, it might simply be drinking lemon juice in water, sitting in a sauna, or maybe doing a juice fast.

DETOX WITHIN FUNCTIONAL MEDICINE

However, within Functional Medicine, detox has a specific definition: it is the process of reducing the body's toxic load by lessening exposure to harmful chemicals we are taking in, while simultaneously implementing nutrition and lifestyle strategies to promote efficient elimination of toxins from the body1.

The first step of detoxification can be done, in part, by lessening the immune system load by removing reactive foods from the diet.

The gold standard for this removal is the aptly named "elimination diet", which is a simplified list of foods to eat and foods to exclude as part of a detox program.

Typically, common allergenic foods and beverages containing corn, soy, wheat/gluten, eggs, dairy, shellfish, and peanuts are omitted from the daily diet in conjunction with caffeine, sugar, alcohol, and red meat for 10 to 28 days, depending on the duration of the program.

In Functional Medicine, the elimination diet is often used as the first line of therapy for immune and gastrointestinal issues since it can help with reducing toxic load and cooling down any immune reactivity to foods.

In conjunction with removal of foods, it's best to take a complementary approach to bolstering the body with specific nutrients to help fortify its pathways of detoxification in the liver, so toxins can be easily removed.

For example, it is well known that certain vitamins and minerals—like B vitamins and iron—are required to assist in the activity of these enzymes.

Coupling nutrients together with an elimination diet (through their inclusion as whole, plant-based foods and as scientifically formulated dietary supplements) is perhaps the most robust protocol for a medical detoxification regimen.

Remember that detox has a very specific and science-based definition within Functional Medicine.

In practice, Functional Medicine programs that modify dietary intake and supplement nutritional co-factors that support the body's endogenous detoxification pathways can mitigate toxic burden to reduce incoming toxic exposures, and, at the same time, equip the body with nutrients known to support the body's natural capacity to shuttle toxins out.

SIDE EFFECTS OF DETOX

The side effects depend on the plan and how long you are on it. You may feel hungry and weak, or have low energy, low blood sugar, dizziness, or lightheadedness.

One of the most common side effects is a headache within the first few days of starting the detox diet, which is often due to caffeine withdrawal.

Proponents often suggest gradually decreasing the amount of caffeine prior to starting a detox diet to avoid caffeine withdrawal symptoms.

In addition, some people opt to start the diet on the weekend.

Other side effects include excessive diarrhea, which can lead to dehydration and electrolyte loss.

Constipation may occur if people consume excess fiber without increasing their fluid intake.

Any worsening of symptoms or new symptoms that occur during a detox diet should prompt a visit to a qualified health professional.

If a detox diet is continued for a longer time, it may result in low body weight and nutrient deficiencies, particularly protein (some diets omit animal products) and calcium.

People who are in recovery and no longer use drugs or alcohol can still experience withdrawal months or years after they have stopped using drugs and alcohol.

This is called Post-Acute Withdrawal Syndrome (PAWS), and it is a set of continuing withdrawal symptoms that affect the person mentally or physically.

They can last a few days when they do occur and they can occur at different times throughout the year.

It is advised that recovering users seek professional help to manage this syndrome if they feel they need or have been professionally advised to do it.

PAWS symptoms do not have to be managed on your own.

Other things that help users in recovery getting past this difficult stage is getting enough rest, practicing habits that promote health and wellness, and having a supportive network of people.

Consult with your personal physician to develop the best plan for you.

People either swoon or cringe when they hear the word "detox."

Those who stand behind it claim it gets rid of their symptoms—everything from brain fog to joint pain and fatigue—while others strongly assert there is no need to detox, and it is just marketing hype. Why such polarized views?

A NOTE ON SUPPLEMENTS

I recommend taking a combination of six different supplements during a gut cleanse. Your health practitioner will confirm which ones are right for you.

Probiotic powder or capsule - this promotes healthy gut bacteria. Look for one that contains at least 15 million CFU and includes Lactobacillus acidophilus, Bifidobacterium lactis and Lactobacillus rhamnosus strains.

Aloe vera and spirulina green powder - these both promote gut cleansing and repairing.

Glutamine powder or capsule - this strengthens and supports gut lining.

Digestive enzymes capsules - these promote optimal food digestion and nutrient absorption.

Fish oil capsules - these have great anti-inflammatory benefits. Look for 1000mg per capsule.

These supplements support digestion and absorption of nutrients, protect and heal gut lining and repopulate good bacteria for bowel health.

If you only took one, I'd suggest a probiotic as our diets often lack probiotic-rich foods. However, you can still do a cleanse without supplements and improve your gut health.

WHAT SHOULD YOU WATCH OUT FOR?

Detox diets are supposedly to help "clean out the system" but many people think they will lose weight if they try these diets. Here's the truth:

Detox diets are not recommended for teens.

Normal teenagers need lots of nutritional goodies — like enough calories and protein to support rapid growth and development.

So diets that involve fasting and severe restriction of food are not a good idea.

Some sports and physical activities require ample food, and fasting does not provide enough fuel to support them.

For these reasons, detox diets can be especially risky for teenagers.

Detox diets aren't for people with health conditions. They're not recommended for people with diabetes, heart disease, or other chronic medical conditions.

Detox diets should be avoided if you are pregnant or have an eating disorder.

Detox diets can be addicting. That's because there's a certain feeling that comes from going without food or from having an enema — for some, it's almost like the high other people get from nicotine or alcohol.

This can become a dangerous addiction that leads to health problems, including serious eating disorders, heart problems, and even death.

Detox supplements can have side effects.

Many of the supplements used during detox diets are actually laxatives, which are designed to make people go to the bathroom more often, and that can get messy.

Laxative supplements are never a good idea because they can cause dehydration, mineral imbalances, and problems with the digestive system.

Detox diets don't help people lose fat. People who fast for several days may drop pounds, but most of it will be water and some of it may be muscle.

Most people regain the weight they lost soon after completing the program.

Detox diets are for short-term purposes only.

In addition to causing other health problems, fasting for long periods can slow down a person's metabolism, making it harder to keep the weight off or to lose weight later.

PREPARATION TO DETOX

Eat ama-reducing foods. Favor vegetarian foods that are lighter, warm, cooked and digestible.

Avoid heavy dairy products such as cheese or yogurt (although lassi is good); foods that are fried or oily; raw foods of any kind; heavy desserts; and foods with refined sugar and honey, as these are harder to digest and create ama.

Avoid breads made with yeast and dry breads such as crackers. Freshly-made flat breads, freshly-made soups and dhals, organic vegetables cooked with spices, and freshly-made grains are ideal.

Certain fruits, vegetables and spices are especially helpful in detoxifying, so you'll want to favor them during detoxification.

Fruits: cooked prunes, figs, apples, pears, pineapple and papaya.

Vegetables: cooked leafy greens, Brussels sprouts and cabbage.

Grains: quinoa, barley, amaranth, rice and kanji (rice water).

Spices: ginger, turmeric, coriander, fennel and fenugreek. These spices help open up the channels and support the flow of toxins from the skin, urinary tract, colon and liver.

Avoid ama-producing foods. In general, you'll want to avoid foods that produce ama, such as leftovers as well as dead foods such as packaged, canned and frozen foods.

You'll also want to avoid foods that create garvisha, such as non-organic foods; foods grown with chemicals, pesticides and chemical fertilizers; and foods with chemical additives.

Choose foods according to your body type or imbalances. This will help regulate your agni (digestive fire).

For more information on diets and foods for pacifying each of the three doshas, visit the foods section.

Drink plenty of hot water throughout the day to flush toxins out of the body through the urine. Or better still, choose one of the detoxifying herbal waters mentioned later in this newsletter.

Massage daily. One of the most important purification procedures in Maharishi Ayurveda is warm oil massage (abhyanga), and you can do it every day on your own.

Abhyanga loosens impurities from the shrotas and tissues, allowing them to flow into the digestive tract, where they can be easily eliminated through the bowel.

While you're detoxifying, take a little extra time with your morning massage, and you'll magnify the results many times.

Get enough rest. You may need more sleep while detoxifying. It's also important to go to bed early (before 10 p.m.) and get up early (before 6 a.m.), as both staying up late and sleeping late in the morning can flood the shrotas (microcirculatory channels) with toxins.

Exercise each day.

Gentle exercise such as Yoga asanas and walking can support detoxification by improving digestion and elimination and moving toxins out of the body.

Walking for twenty minutes or half an hour is ideal, because it allows you to breathe deeply, purify the respiratory system and supply the cells with cleansing prana. Walking in the early morning especially helps move toxins out of the body.

Yoga asanas are designed to purify and enliven different organs of the body, and they also enhance digestion and elimination, as does all exercise.

Pranayama breathing exercises are also excellent for cleansing the respiratory system and other organs. During the preparation for detox and the actual self-detox program, it's best to avoid strenuous exercise.

Use warm oil massage with herbs added, such as Youthful Skin Massage Oil for Men and for Women, as the herbs are chosen to penetrate the surface of the skin and reach the deeper layers and tissues, purifying and nourishing the shrotas of the skin.

By gently massaging the whole body, you're also gently purifying other organs as well. Increasing circulation also helps purify the blood.

Always follow your abhyanga with a warm (not hot) bath. Purifying Therapeutic Bath Salts, a blend of natural salts and the essential oils of Niaoli, Sandalwood and Eucalytpus, can be added to your bath to draw out the toxins. If you don't have time for a bath, a shower can substitute.

Detox to Balance Hormones

Anyone looking to balance hormones has tried a diet to help them get their hormones back on track. However, balancing your hormones with diet alone might not be getting you the results you really need. That's where a holistic detox comes in!

I recommend women in my medical practice detox if they are experiencing acne, hormonal headaches, symptoms of estrogen dominance, have a thyroid condition, struggle with adrenal dysfunction or other signs of a hormone imbalance.

By supporting the liver and other organs of elimination, your body can effectively excrete excess hormones, metabolic waste and environmental toxins.

When people say, "You should detox" or "I'm detoxing" what does that really mean?

Most commonly what we Naturopathic and Functional Medicine Doctors are referring to when we say "detox" is not only the reduction of incoming toxins, but also the body's basic physiological process of metabolizing chemicals, hormones, toxicants, and other environmental compounds to a less toxic or harmful form.

Whew! That's a mouthful, huh?

The basic premise is to support your organs of elimination, those organs which detox and remove waste from the body — liver, kidneys, gut, lymphatic system, lungs, skin, and sweat glands.

The Most Common Ways to Detox

There are many ways to do a detox diet, ranging from total starvation fasts and juicing to simpler food modifications.

Most detox diets involve at least one of the following (1):

Fasting for 1–3 days.

Drinking fresh fruit and vegetable juices, smoothies, water and tea.

Drinking only specific liquids, such as salted water or lemon juice.

Eliminating foods high in heavy metals, contaminants and allergens.

Taking supplements or herbs.

Avoiding all allergenic foods, and then slowly reintroducing them.

Using laxatives, colon cleanses or enemas.

Exercising regularly.

Completely eliminating alcohol, coffee, cigarettes and refined sugar.

The different detox diets vary in intensity and duration.

There are many kinds of detoxes. Some of them involve fasting, eating specific foods, avoiding harmful ingredients and taking supplements.

WHICH TOXINS ARE ELIMINATED?

Detox diets rarely identify the specific toxins they aim to remove or how exactly they eliminate them.

In fact, there is little to no evidence that detox diets actually remove any "toxins" from your body.

More importantly, there is really no scientific evidence backing up the claim that our bodies are loaded with toxins and need to be cleansed.

Your body is actually very capable of cleansing itself, through the liver, feces, urine and sweat. The liver makes toxic substances harmless and then makes sure they're released from the body.

Despite this, there are a few chemicals that may not be as easily removed by these processes, including persistent organic pollutants, pthalates, bisphenol A (BPA) and heavy metals.

These tend to accumulate in fat tissue or blood and can take a very long time, even years, for the body to get rid of.

However, generally speaking, these compounds are removed from or limited in commercial products today.

All that being said, there is little evidence that detox diets actually help remove any of these compounds.

Detox diets rarely identify the specific toxins they're removing, and there is little evidence that they even remove any toxins. Your body can clear itself of most toxins through the liver, feces, urine and sweat.

Does Detox Really Work?

Some people report feeling more focused and energetic during and after detox diets.

However, this improved well-being may simply be due to eliminating processed foods, alcohol and other unhealthy substances from your diet.

You may also be getting vitamins and minerals that were lacking before.

On the other hand, many people also report feeling very unwell during the detox period.

There is some evidence from animal studies that indicates coriander, an algae called Chlorella, and several types of fruit acids and pectin may help eliminate toxic metals and organic pollutants.

Don't Put Junk in Your Body

People encounter toxic substances all the time.

Most of the time, your body does a perfectly good job of removing them without any additional help.

However, if doing a detox diet makes you start eating and feeling better, then it is a great thing.

But this probably has nothing to do with eliminating toxins, but simply the fact that you're putting less junk in your body.

A much smarter approach is to avoid putting toxic things (junk food, cigarette smoke, etc) in your body in the first place.

If you don't "tox" then there's no need to detox!

Cleanse vs. Detox

No doubt, you've heard of juice cleanses, sugar cleanses, and detox diets.

And if you've ever tried to break a weight-loss plateau, beat the bloat, or get back on track after a little too much mac and cheese, someone has probably suggested doing a body cleanse or detox diet (also known as a detox cleanse) to get things going again.

Cleansing and detoxing are getting a ton of hype right now — do a Google search for "detox" or "cleanse" and you'll get millions of results. Turns out you can pretty much cleanse or detox almost every aspect of your life.

You could use them end toxic relationships, block toxic trolls on social media, or do a "digital detox" to break your screen habit.

When it comes to body cleanses and detoxes, the amount of info out there is overwhelming.

But doing a cleanse or detox diet is more than just unfriending a bully or unplugging your iPad. It can affect your health and nutrition, so it's important to dig deeper to figure out the truth behind the hype.

There are key differences between a cleanse and a detox diet, but people tend to use the two terms interchangeably, which makes things even more confusing. So what's the difference between a cleanse and a detox? Read on to find out.

Your Body Detoxifies Itself

Assuming you don't fall face first into a radioactive swamp, your body is equipped to deal with most toxins. When you inhale, ingest, or absorb toxins, your liver and kidneys work to flush many of them out — and they've been doing this long before cleanses and detoxes came about.

But if you're constantly hammering yourself with environmental toxins and skimping on nutrients and proper hydration, your body's natural detoxification system can be inhibited.

"Your body wants to get rid of the unhealthy stuff, but if you keep eating more junk, you're not going to be able to get the other junk out," says Denis Faye, M.S. and Beachbody's executive director of nutrition. "It's like clogging a drain."

It puts your liver and kidneys under a lot of pressure — and that's where cleansing comes in.

WHAT ARE TOXINS?

When people talk about body cleanses or detox diets, they talk about the dangers of "toxins" a lot, but usually in a very non-specific way: Toxins are all around us! Your body is filled with toxins that need to be flushed out!

But what exactly are these toxins?

Toxins are potentially harmful substances we come into contact with every day — pesticides on your produce, pollutants in the air, unpronounceable ingredients in processed food, or heavy metals like mercury and arsenic in the soil, to name just a few.

You've probably also heard that foods like gluten, dairy, and refined sugar are "toxic" — but unless you have an allergy or intolerance, you don't have to swear off bread forever.

While anything can be toxic if you consume too much of it, the occasional handful of cookies won't turn you into a biohazard. That said, if you're eating a ton of sugar, you might want to consider cutting back, like Beachbody Editor Hannah Rex did when she went on a sugar cleanse and gave up sweets and added sugars for three weeks.

But especially in our modern world, many of us are constantly bombarded by toxins in the air, in food, in our cleaning products, everywhere — and those toxins can add up.

What Is a Cleanse?

There are two Beachbody cleanses: the 3-Day Refresh and the 21-day Ultimate Reset. These cleanse diets don't just eliminate junk from your diet — they also focus on fueling your body with nutrient-rich foods that support your natural detoxification processes.

"Fluids, fiber, and phytonutrients from fruits and vegetables can go a long way in terms of supporting your wellness and your body's natural systems," Faye says.

By stripping your diet down to the essentials, you're giving your liver and kidneys a chance to do their job more efficiently.

While you'll probably shed a few pounds in the process, the real goal of the Beachbody cleanses is to reshape the way you think about nutrition.

The 3-Day Refresh is a 3-day cleanse that could be a good way to jumpstart a healthy eating plan or help your body recover from a not-so-virtuous weekend; Ultimate Reset is a longer, more intensive program that can help transform your diet in the long run.

But don't jump willy-nilly into a program: It's important to do research and preparation ahead of time so you know what to expect before and after you do it. And while you will have to make some food sacrifices, believe it or not, you won't have to give up flavor or variety.

Talk to your health practitioner for your own plan.

Water - At least 2 litres of spring water and herbal teas throughout the day.

Morning supplements - 1 serve aloe vera + spirulina green powder + 1 serve glutamine powder in 200ml pure water +

2 fish oil capsules + 1 serve digestive enzymes

Breakfast - Quinoa and grated pear porridge cooked with almond milk and 1 tbs flaxseed meal + 100g unsweetened natural yogurt

Snack - Handful raw nuts + green tea

Lunch - Mixed seasonal vegetable salad with a palm serve size of grilled organic / free range chicken seasoned with garlic, tamari soy and turmeric powder.

Dressing 1 tbsp. apple cider vinegar + 1 tbsp. extra virgin cold pressed olive oil

More about Apple Cider Vinegar:

Apple Cider Vinegar: Lose Weight, Detox, and Cleanse to Heal

Snack - Raw vegetables + guacamole (mashed avocado, chopped tomato, lemon juice, garlic, coriander and seasoning)

Dinner - Palm serve size of baked salmon with seasonal baked vegetables with coconut oil + side serve of kimchi

Evening supplements - 1 serve aloe vera + spirulina green powder + 1 serve glutamine powder in 200ml pure water +

2 fish oil capsules + 1 serve probiotics

WHICH IS BETTER AFTER BINGE DRINKING?

A night of heavy drinking can cause a large accumulation of chemicals like ethanol and its metabolites in the blood stream. These chemicals are toxic in large enough doses, and are the reason you can die from alcohol poisoning if they aren't filtered out of your system.

This filtration is carried out by the liver and kidneys, so naturally, a detox diet works best here. This can be done through a detox water diet or through a convention detox type program.

Studies have actually shown that certain herbal ingredients not only helped increase the speed of alcohol excretion but also reduced the severity of a hangover.

So, to help you recover both physically and psychologically from a hangover, a morning alcohol detox could work wonders.

How often should you cleanse?

This depends on your symptoms but generally you should commit to a cleanse once or twice a year, under the care of a health professional.

Post-antibiotic treatment is a must, as you need to nourish the gut and replace all of the healthy bacteria that's been wiped out by antibiotics.

After holidays is also a good time to cleanse as alcohol and treat foods wreak havoc on gut bacteria and gut lining.

Post-cleanse you should continue to include gut-friendly foods and nutrients as a part of your regular diet.

WHICH IS BETTER TO DETOX THE LIVER?

This may seem obvious from the name of the scenario, but the truth is, because both programs can be healthier than the average western diet, both could help improve the health of your liver.

However, a **detox diet is the clear winner here**.

The right detox diet will help protect your liver from breakdown and increase its efficiency to help it clear all the toxins and metabolites from your body.

Your liver represents the human body's primary filtration system, converting toxins into waste products, cleansing your blood, and metabolizing nutrients and medications to provide the body with some of its most important proteins.

As such a fundamental part of the body's overall regulation, it's paramount to keep your liver healthy and to limit overindulgence.

In recent years, many products have flooded the market purporting to detox and cleanse your liver, whether it's after a weekend of bingeing on food or alcohol, to maintain daily liver function, or to repair an already damaged liver.

Though liver cleanses are packaged to claim that they're a cure-all for daily liver health and overindulgence, I do not recommend them.

While some common ingredients in liver cleanses have been shown to have positive results — milk thistle has been shown to decrease liver inflammation, and turmeric extract has been shown to protect against liver injury — there have not been adequate clinical trial data in humans to recommend the routine use of these natural compounds for prevention.

As for overindulgence of alcohol or food, less is always best when it comes to liver health, and cleanses have not been proven to rid your body of damage from excess consumption.

Many liver detoxification products are also sold as weight loss cleanses.

However, there are no clinical data to support the efficacy of these cleanses. In fact, some dietary supplements can actually cause harm to the liver by leading to drug-induced injury and should thus be used with caution.

Here are a few types of liver disease and their available treatment options:

Hepatitis A and B. You should be vaccinated against hepatitis A and B if you are not immune or have any other underlying liver disease. Highly effective oral medications for patients with chronic hepatitis B infection are available as well.

Alcoholic liver disease. All alcohol consumption should cease in order to allow the liver the best chance for recovery.

The liver has an amazing ability to regenerate and heal once active injury has been stopped.

Hepatitis C. Highly effective, well-tolerated oral medications now exist to treat hepatitis C.

Nonalcoholic fatty liver disease. The most effective treatment for nonalcoholic fatty liver disease is weight loss, which has been shown to decrease the amount of fat in the liver and the inflammation caused by the fat.

The following measures are recommended:

Do not drink alcohol in excess.

On a routine basis, men should not consume more than three drinks per day, and women should not consume more than two drinks per day to prevent the development of alcoholic liver disease.

Avoid weight gain. Maintain your body mass index in the normal range (18 to 25) by eating healthy and exercising on a regular basis to decrease your risk of developing nonalcoholic fatty liver disease.

Beware engaging in risky behaviors.

To avoid the risk of acquiring viral hepatitis, do not engage in behaviors such as illicit drug use or having unprotected sex with multiple partners.

Know your risk factors. If you have the following risk factors for liver disease, it's important to go for screening, as chronic liver disease can be silent for years and go unrecognized:

WHICH IS BETTER TO BOOST ENERGY LEVELS? BOTH.

This is a more difficult question to answer.

While both diets can be beneficial for this aim, the detox diet may prove slightly more beneficial due to the low calorie and intermittent fasting style of the diet.

While the cleanse can be useful, some people may experience an initial period of low energy due to the reduction in carbohydrates.

For a more immediate boost in energy levels, a detox water diet may prove more useful.

WHICH IS BETTER TO DETOX THE KIDNEYS?

This is another scenario that, while seeming obvious, can benefit from either type of protocol.

However, kidney detoxification will benefit more from a detox water diet, which will increase urination, help decrease the risk of urinary tract infections and increase the speed at which chemicals are excreted from the body.

Cleansing your liver of alcohol is one of the essential steps in recovering from alcoholism, excessive alcohol consumptions or prolonged alcohol abuse.

The liver is critically involved in all metabolic processes in the body. It breaks down old blood cells, promotes blood clotting, breaks down fats into energy, and removes toxins from the body.

Kidneys also release three important hormones: erythropoietin (which stimulates the bone marrow to make red blood cells), renin (which regulates blood pressure), and calcitriol (the active form of vitamin D, which helps maintain calcium for bones and for normal chemical balance in the body).

If you consume adequate fluids, which can take the form of foods such as fruits and vegetables as well as water and other liquids, the kidneys are self-cleansing.

A number of products, foods, or specialized diets (typically marketed under the term "kidney cleanse") claim to detoxify the kidneys in order to promote healthy kidney function and prevent kidney stones.

Kidney cleanses are also purported to help keep blood pressure in check, improve the functioning of the urinary tract and bladder, boost immunity, and clear toxins from the entire body.

Although the individual components of a kidney cleanse (such as certain herbs, foods, or nutrients) may offer health benefits, there's no scientific evidence to support their use in cleansing the kidneys or preventing kidney stones or infection.

If you're interested in taking natural approaches to enhancing your kidney health, talk with your doctor and consider consulting a qualified health professional.

While kidney-cleanse proponents suggest that they enhance the kidneys' ability to remove waste from the body, their claims are not backed by scientific data. Like other supplements, the Food and Drug Administration (FDA) doesn't require products marketed for kidney cleansing be proven safe and effective.

While consumers face such risks when purchasing any dietary supplement, these risks may be of greater magnitude with supplements containing a variety of herbs in high doses.

Pregnant or nursing women and children and people with kidney disease shouldn't try a kidney cleanse.

You can get tips on using supplements, but if you're considering the use of a kidney cleanse or supplement, talk with your primary care provider first.

Avoiding or delaying standard care can have serious consequences.

Which is better to boost mental health?

Improving mental health is another area where both diets do a good job through different means.

While the detox water ingredients help deliver some essential and highly beneficial nutrients, cleanse diets help improve gut health, which has a surprisingly big effect on mental health.

However, the detox water diet can take the edge in this scenario too, due to its high nutrient content and low calories, both of which can encourage cell growth in the brain and may improve mental health and well-being.

WHAT ARE THE PROS AND CONS OF DETOXING?

Before you decide to cleanse and spend big bucks on a magic drink or pounds of freshly juiced fruits and vegetables, be sure to weigh the benefits and drawbacks.

Pros:

You'll benefit from increased intake of vitamins and minerals either naturally from juiced fruits and veggies or supplemented from drinks

It can help you identify food sensitivities by eliminating certain foods for several days, then gradually reintroducing potential trigger foods

Cons:

These diets are low in calories, which will leave you with little energy to exercise and may disrupt your metabolic rate and blood glucose levels

You may experience gastrointestinal distress and frequent bowel movements

Detox diets are low in protein

Whatever you decide, remember that your body is meant to detox itself. A balanced diet of whole foods such as vegetables, fruit, whole grains and legumes is healthy for your entire body and won't interfere with your ability to exercise.

The Purpose of Detoxing and Cleansing

The Purpose of Detoxing:

When you detox, the goal is to get toxins like cigarette residue, heavy metals, chemicals, or environmental toxins out the body via waste elimination.

Secondly, it's important to improve the body's detoxification pathways, specifically the liver and the kidneys.

Those organs are always detoxing, so a "detox" is a way to make sure those organs are functioning without problems.

A detox also involves a dietary change.

THE PURPOSE OF CLEANSING:

The primary purpose of a cleanse is to remove undigested food, toxins, old fecal matter, and parasites from the digestive tract and colon.

When you are cleansing, you typically have to avoid consuming dairy products, eggs, gluten, soy, refined sugars, meats, processed foods, and alcohol.

The goal is to focus on foods that aid the cleansing process, yet supply the body with tons of nutrients as well.

The Whole Body Cleanse

We live in a toxic world. Toxins come from many sources, including pollution, pesticides and fertilizers, hormones used in raising livestock, processed foods and other sources in our air, food and water.

The vast amount of toxins in our environment can create a real challenge for the build-in detoxification system in your body.

Whole body leanse can help you rejuvenate, refortify and detoxify your body.

I try my best to educate people that the human body has a natural ability to detoxify itself. In fact, the body has several systems in place for removing waste.

The excretory system plays the largest role in detoxification. The most obvious job of this system is defecation and urination.

The main organs that compose the excretory system are the skin, liver, lungs, large intestine, and kidneys.

You may be surprised to learn that your skin is part of your excretory system, but it's true---the skin aids in elimination through the sweat glands.

The purpose of sweat is to regulate body temperature, but it's a multifunctional system. When sweat passes through your sweat glands, it takes toxins with it.

The roles of the other organs are just as important. It's the liver's job to filter and excrete waste, hormones, drugs, and other foreign substances.

The lungs help remove carbon dioxide (the waste gas resulting from breathing).

The large intestine has several important jobs. It absorbs water and remaining nutrients from food. It also converts waste into stool to be expelled from the body through defecation.

The kidneys filter the blood and help remove waste from the body through urination.

The entire body relies on this system to live a healthy life. Your body is detoxifying itself all the time, around the clock, 24/7.

Even your brain flushes out toxins while you sleep.It's essential to take care of these organs and allow them to do their job.

Choose the Right Foods

One of the best things you can do to support your body's detoxification process is to lighten its load and decrease the toxins you put in your body in the first place.

Choose organic vegetables and fruits over fast food and other processed foods.

GMO products and pesticide contaminated foods add harmful toxins to your diet.

Avoid them like the plague.

Vegetables

Vegetables are rich in phytochemicals (naturally-occurring plant chemicals) that are being explored for their potential to regulate hormones, stimulate the immune system, and prevent damage to our body's cells.

A good rule of thumb is to incorporate vegetables into most meals, filling at least half of each plate with a variety of brightly colored (or strongly flavored) vegetables.

Vegetables thought to be particularly good for a liver detox include onions, garlic, beets, artichokes, and cruciferous vegetables like broccoli, cauliflower, cabbage, collard greens, kale, and Brussels sprouts.

Other vegetables to eat include asparagus, carrots, celery, cucumbers, endives, jicama, kohlrabi, leeks, lettuce, okra, parsnips, radishes, rutabaga, snow peas, spinach, sprouts, squash, sweet potatoes, turnips, watercress, yams, yucca, zucchini, and sea vegetables including arame, dulse, hijiki, kelp, nori sheets, and wakame.

Fats

During a cleanse, focus on fats from foods like avocado, raw nuts and seeds, coconut, and nut and seed butter:

Almonds

- Brazil nut
- Cashew
- Chia
- Hazelnut
- Hemp seeds, hemp nuts, hemp hearts
- Macadamia Nut
- Pecan
- Pine nut
- Pistachio
- Pumpkin
- Sesame seeds
- Sunflower seeds
- Flax seeds
- Poppy Seeds
- Walnuts
- Coconut

Nut and seed butter, such as tahini, almond butter, cashew nut butter

If you're cooking with oil, try to use high-quality, cold-pressed, unrefined oils, such as:

- Olive oil
- Hemp oil
- Flax oil
- Almond oil
- Avocado oil
- Coconut oil
- Hazelnut oil
- Pumpkin oil
- Walnut oil

Safflower, sesame, and sunflower oils in limited amounts.

Fruit

Like vegetables, fruit contain phytonutrients that may provide health benefits. Aim for five to 10 servings of colorful fruits and vegetables per day.

Choose whole fruit (fresh or frozen), such as apples, apricots, blackberries, blueberries, cantaloupe, cherries, cranberries, grapefruit, figs, grapes, guava, kiwi, lemon, lime, loganberries, mango, melon, nectarines, oranges, papaya, peaches, pears, pineapple, plums, pomegranate, prunes, raspberries, strawberries, tangerines, and watermelon.

Whole Grains and Complex Carbs

Everyone has their go-to carbs (often pasta and bread), but this is a good time to experiment and try other sources of whole grains and complex carbs, such as:

- Rice
- Quinoa
- Barley
- Buckwheat
- Farro
- Freekeh
- Millet
- Amaranth
- Wild rice
- Teff
- Tapioca
- Arrowroot
- Oats
- Winter squash
- Sweet potato

Unrefined whole grains are preferred, but also try products made from the above ingredients, including brown rice pasta, buckwheat soba noodles, glass noodles, kelp noodles, mung bean noodles, shirataki noodles, rice crackers, quinoa flakes, gluten-free bread, and rice bran.

Beverages

In general, it's a good idea to use your thirst to guide how much you drink, although some people have conditions that may require them to drink more or less.

You may decide to limit your alcohol and coffee intake, swapping in herbal, green, or white tea. Here are some beverage options:

Infused water (sometimes called "detox water")

Plant-based "milks" such as rice milk, almond milk, hemp milk.

Coconut water

Lemon water

Herbal teas, such as rooibos, cinnamon tea, ginger tea

Green tea, white tea

Kombucha (unsweetened)

Unsweetened juice made from allowed fruits and vegetables

Mineral or seltzer water

Drinks or smoothies with allowed ingredients

If you simply can't give up your morning cup of coffee, try limiting it to no more than one 8-ounce cup (and avoid added sweetener).

Condiments

Fresh and dried herbs and spices can make any meal more flavorful, without adding sugar or salt.

Chop some fresh herbs such as basil, chives, cilantro, dill, mint, oregano, parsley, rosemary, sage, tarragon, or thyme.

Spices you can cook with include allspice, anise, caraway seeds, cardamom, celery seeds, cinnamon, cloves, coriander, cumin, nutmeg, saffron, tamarind, or turmeric.

Fresh or raw ginger and garlic can instantly make meals more interesting.

Here are some other condiments and ingredients to consider:

- Vinegar (e.g. apple cider vinegar, balsamic, coconut, red or white wine, rice vinegar)
- Baking soda or baking powder
- Coconut amino acids
- Fish sauce
- Nama shoyu
- Nutritional yeast
- Miso
- Olives

Beans and Legumes

Beans and legumes are high in fiber, protein, and iron. They're also less expensive than animal protein. Try:

Split yellow and green peas

Lentils (red, brown, green, yellow, French, du Puy)

Other beans and legumes, such as adzuki, cannellini, chickpeas, black, black-eyed peas, kidney, and lima.

Exercise and Meditation

Exercise and meditation help maintain a healthy body.

Exercising helps you sweat, and sweating helps release toxins through your skin. Studies have found trace amounts of arsenic, cadmium, lead, and mercury in sweat.

Meditation helps you clear your mind and reduce stress.

Read also: The Power of Meditation: Essential strategies to deep relaxation, positive thinking, self-discipline, and inspiration

Stress can be as toxic to your health as chemicals.

A troubled mind can cause the physical body to function poorly.

In order to build a sequence for detoxing, it's important to look at the systems of the body that we can help detoxify, and which classes of asana target those systems. Then, all we have to do is pick a few poses from each asana group, and before you know it, you've got a meaningful and powerful practice to boost your body's already boomin' detoxing processes. (You can check The Complete Guide to Yoga: The Best Yoga Poses for Beginners for more information)

Diet

Detoxifying your body is not only about what you avoid, but also about what you consume. Following a healthy diet can go a long way. There are also many foods that aid detoxification — garlic, lemon, broccoli sprouts, mung beans, and raw vegetables.

Many diets promote cleansing and detoxification. I follow and recommend an organic, variable, intermittent fasting diet but there are other options if that isn't for you.

You could also try a raw alkaline diet. It's a temporary cleanse consisting of uncooked fruits and vegetables and raw nuts, seeds, and sprouts. It's a great strategy for detoxing the colon and liver.

A juice diet is also helpful and is centered around consuming freshly-made fruit and vegetable juice—preferably organic.

PURIFY THE AIR YOU BREATHE

Breathing clean air is another way to reduce your exposure to toxins.

While you can't control the whole environment, you can control the air in your home.

Smoke, fumes, pet dander, mold, mildew, and microorganisms can make the air in your home more toxic than the air outside.

A high-quality air purification device is the best way to keep your air fresh and toxin-free.

If a quality air purification device is out of your budget, get a few house plants instead; they're nature's air fresheners.

They help filter the air and remove toxins.

It also promotes the creation of white blood cells.

Every time you inhale your lungs fill with oxygen that thereafter get transported in your blood throughout other detoxing organs including: lymphatic system, kidneys, colon, and even the uterus for women.

Conversely every time we exhale we elimate part of the body's waste in the form of carbon dioxide.

By breathing deeply we take in more oxygen that cleanses the body, and by exhaling deeply we eliminate more waste both actions have an overall detox effect on the body.

We often take breathing for granted and under estimate the importance of drawing awareness to our breath.

However, this can result in shallow breathing with side effects that include fatigue, and decreased tissue function.

Additionally the brain can not function to it's fullest potential if it is not receiving enough oxygen.

When you practice deep rhythmic breathing the diaphragm expands. It relaxes the body, and massages your lymphatic system which helps in the elimination of toxins.

If you aren't breathing deeply or moving on a regular basis your lymphatic fluids become stagnant and this essential blocks the system from eliminating waste.

A poorly functioning lymphatic system can lead to high blood pressure, heart problems, weight gain, fatigue, and inflammation.

Learning to breath deeply is an easy process.

Breathing affects all of our bodily systems, feelings, and moods in profound ways.

In an age where most humans are in a constant state of anxiety—an over-activation of the sympathetic nervous system—proper breathing provides a healthy means of reducing anxiety, restlessness, and stress.

By activating the parasympathetic nervous system, proper breathing promotes inner calm and physical relaxation.

The brain uses up to three times as much oxygen as our muscles do.

Proper breathing increases the oxygen in our bloodstream, making more oxygen available to our brains.

This improves brain function, which translates to more physical energy, mental clarity, and greater productivity.

By learning to direct your attention to your breath, you can condition yourself to shift out of stressful, depressed, and aggressive states and enter relaxed, calm, and resourceful mental states.

The short-term benefits are obvious: you become better equipped at handling difficult situations, managing conflicts, and maintaining focus while you work.

Because effective breathing improves your body's response to stress, its long-term benefits include longevity and a higher quality of life.

Once you get accustomed to deep breathing exercises your day to day breathing will become less shallow and allow your body to work more efficiently.

Take a few minutes a day to focus on you inhalation and exhalation. Inhale deeply until you feel you belly full of air, hold your breath for 2-3 seconds and exhale slowly and deeply until all air is expelled.

Breathing properly can be a huge way to update your overall health.

In fact, breathing is the bridge between mind and body, and the connection between consciousness and unconsciousness.

What makes this human function even more powerful, is that it's the only one we perform both consciously and unconsciously.

It's controlled by two sets of nerves – one which belongs to the voluntary nervous system and the other to the autonomic system.

Simply breathing more deeply helps lower your blood pressure, calm your heart rate, and aid in your digestion too.

Even more, it has a deep and direct connection to our emotional state and mood.

Notice yourself when you feel angry or upset. How is your breathing?

Typically, you will find short, shallow breathing as a result of this mood shift.

We can actually alter our mood by changing the way we breathe!

In fact, you cannot be upset if your breathing is slow, deep, and consistent.

Purify Your Body With Water

Water is possibly the most valuable tool for detoxifying your body. The body's most basic functions require water.

Your body needs water to produce saliva, help with perspiration, and remove waste.

When I say drink water, I do mean water, not coffee, or sports drinks, or soft drinks. If you're one of those people that find the taste of water boring, try adding lemon or cucumber to your water.

Whether you are religious or not, water blesses and cleanses the soul. Without water there is no life. Water is energy, and energy is life.

You are made up of mainly water, the planet is 70 percent water, life is created from water, and life can be healed from water. Your body and soul craves hydrotherapy as a means of promoting wellness and healing.

Water evokes purity, clarity and calmness. It's nature's way of helping you cleanse your mind, body and soul.

Water is one of the most vital elements of life, yet it is probably the one thing that many of us take for granted.

Many of us are dehydrated; not only do we not drink enough of this miracle elixir, we mindlessly shower in it, curse it when it falls from the sky and run from it when it tries to weep from our bodies.

The humble drop of water enables us to see vibrant rainbow colors reflecting in the sunlight, it gives shape and form to everything, it builds mountains and cliffs, it floods our bodies with nourishment, and it helps to release the pain within our body through the tears we cry.

As a surfer, I have grown up with a connection to water. Over the years I have turned to water as my healer on several occasions.

The grey and angry waves that have crushed me have humbled my soul, the unpredictable moods of the ocean have taught me to respect and never to assume, and with every wave I have been fortunate enough to ride, I have been filled with gratitude.

We all have this innate knowing that water is healing, however only some of us listen to our own wisdom and knowing.

To prove this theory, take a moment now to think about relaxation and rejuvenation. Create visions in your mind of the perfect relaxation scene. What is it?

I am almost certain that at least 80 percent of you would have envisioned one of these scenes:

- Relaxing on a tropical island surrounded in turquoise calm waters
- Soaking in a hot bath
- Swimming in a beautiful freshwater lake
- Walking on a pristine beach or swimming in the gentle ocean
- Getting lost by the beauty and tranquility of a waterfall
- Being rocked by the gentle sounds of the rolling waves
- Being stirred by the trickling of water from a water fountain or Zen garden
- And all the many other magical experiences that include water….

So there you have it. When you are seeking a little relaxation, you intuitively connect with the energy of water.

The healing powers of water deeply resonate within your soul, you have an inner connection and knowing that water is the essence of life.

Water isn't the only way to meet your fluid needs. All drinks, including low-fat milk and 100 percent fruit juices, help up your fluid intake.

Caffeinated beverages, like coffee and tea, increase your fluid level as well. But caffeine can have a diuretic effect, making you urinate excessively and ultimately leaving you dehydrated if you have excessive amounts. Moisture-rich food such as soups, fruits and vegetables are other sources of water.

Foods actually make up roughly 20 percent of the water you have in your diet.

While you might think that guzzling bottles of water all day long will help flush out your system even more, it is possible to go way overboard.

Too much water imbalances the electrolytes in your body as your blood becomes diluted.

This condition, called hyponatremia, leads to weakened muscles, an irregular heartbeat, brain swelling and possibly death in rare occurrences. If your urine is very light yellow to clear, it might be time to put the cap on the bottle and stop drinking for a bit.

Your kidneys filter out a lot of toxins in your body. Some of those toxins are simply byproducts of digestion, while others are chemical components of the foods and drinks you take in. But for kidneys as well as the rest of your digestive system to be able to function properly and flush out your system, you need a certain amount of water each day.

Every day we do a variety of things: breathe air that is not so pure, drink liquids that are not so good, etc., which eventually clogs our body filters, such as the lungs, nose, liver, and kidneys.

Over time, our bodies heat up and then the immune system gets knocked down. Fevers actually make the body sweat out toxins and triggers the urge to not eat, a natural fast. Three to four days of water fasting is good in such times. This will help clean out your system.

So should you allow your body to just go through this natural process of getting really sick and going through pain in order to thoroughly cleanse the system? Well, if you are cleaning the filters on a regular basis by doing a water fast, there is no need to get sick.

Kidney Cleanse

Your kidneys are among the most important organs in your body.

They work hard every day detoxifying the blood and sending waste toxins out through the urinary system. Kidneys also balance electrolytes, regulate minerals, like calcium, and help maintain a healthy blood pressure.

With all this work to do and with so many chemicals in our environment, it's not surprising that one in three Americans is at risk of developing kidney disease in their lifetime or that 10 percent of Americans will develop painful kidney stones.

It is not often that you hear people preaching about kidney health, let alone the importance of cleansing them, but the truth is that your kidneys control far more than you might expect. In fact, they are at the root of our health.

Our kidneys determine how we look and feel, both emotionally and physically, from the way our hair and nails grow, to our zest for life. It's all linked back to our kidneys.

This is why their neglect could be the achilles heel for many, preventing transformation in health, especially when everything else seems to be in place.

The kidneys' main functions, from a western perspective, are to keep the body's acid-alkaline and fluid-electrolyte balance, blood volume and pressure control, vitamin D utilization and waste excretion.

While these are vital to the overall functioning of the body, it is their role from a Chinese medicine perspective that highlights their deeper importance and leads us to consider that the kidneys may be holding us back from the health we seek, rather then other aspects such as hormones, liver or digestive function.

Through this perspective, it is believed that the kidneys are intimately tied to the adrenal glands, so much so that they are one in the same, conceptually.

What affects the kidneys affects the adrenal glands, which further deepens their significance to overall wellness.

As the root of life, the kidneys are home of the jing, which is the essence of our life force. It is this life force that is responsible for providing the tools required to fulfill our deepest human needs: survival and reproduction, life and death.

This is what makes kidney cleansing so vital to overall health, because it helps to preserve the jing and the maintenance of its related functions.

Boost Your Metabolism Naturally

Looking for natural ways to raise your metabolism? Your metabolism is the sum of processes that make your body run. Everyone has a basal metabolic rate, which is the number of calories your body burns to keep alive, including breathing and maintaining the required body temperature.

Certain things can increase how many calories your body needs in a day, primarily exercise of various types. Most people think that your weight is just calories in minus calories out, but the truth is that according to the latest science, your metabolic rate can be altered without using medications or other unnatural means.

This is why you can go on certain diets on which you eat more calories and more fat, but still lose weight, like most low-carb diets, such as keto diets or Atkins.

Read also: How to Speed Up Metabolism: The Home Guide to Increase Metabolism for Fast Weight Loss and Muscle Growth

How Does Olive Oil Support Liver Cleansing?

Toxins and chemicals are the root cause of almost any serious health concern, and your liver is no different. Liver cleansing, when done correctly, can help flush the liver of accumulated bile, toxins, and chemicals.

Additionally, relieving your liver of harmful organisms will help you maintain a healthy body and mind. While there are different variations of organic liver cleansing regimens, nearly all take advantage of one key component—olive oil.

Your liver plays a central role in detoxifying your body by keeping your blood clean and free of damaging chemicals and toxins.

The primary duty your liver performs is filtering the blood that comes from your digestive tract. From the liver, blood flows to the rest of your body. Your liver also metabolizes alcohol and prescription drugs.

As your liver performs these critical functions, it produces and releases bile to aid in digestion. When your liver is healthy it releases and safely passes the bile from the body on a regular basis.

The main advantage of performing a liver cleanse is getting rid of the excess bile that builds up over time. Your liver health often depends on your diet and lifestyle.

If you eat clean, non-GMO foods and live a healthy lifestyle, then your liver will show it.

If you live a mainly sedentary lifestyle and consume fatty, unhealthy, or toxic foods, then your liver may be overworked and bogged down.

People with bad diets and exercise habits will experience the greatest benefit from doing a liver cleanse. Some people even feel lighter and slimmer following the cleanse.

HEALTHY OILS

While there are many healthy oils out there with great nutritional benefits, stick with olive oil for natural liver cleanses.

People have tried to substitute with coconut oil, but olive oil remains the most beneficial oil for liver cleansing because of how predictably it works.

When choosing an olive oil to use for a cleanse it is important to select something that is minimally processed.

Look for extra virgin olive oil that comes from fresh olives and does not use heat or chemicals to produce the oil.

Freshness is important when choosing the best olive oil. Even under the right storage conditions, olive oil can degrade and lose nutritional benefits the longer it sits.

Avoid olive oil that is more than two years old. Instead, choose the freshest olive oil you can find.

Day of the Cleanse

On the day of the liver cleanse, eat only fruits and veggies for breakfast, lunch, and dinner.

A few hours before you go to sleep—try for around 7 p.m.—it will be time for the Epsom salts.

Mix one tablespoon of Epsom salt with eight ounces of distilled water and drink. Be aware that loose or liquid stools may happen around 20-30 minutes after drinking the mixture. Immediately before bed—try for around 10 pm—drink six ounces of the extra virgin olive oil and immediately lie in bed on your right side for 30 minutes.

After that, you can go to sleep like normal. The next day you should pass the bile and may even see liver stones in your bowel movements.

If your bowels are not moving, waste will create toxicity and impede health, especially estrogen by-products since estrogen is metabolized in the liver and excreted into the digestive system in the bile.

The bacteria in the large bowel further the breakdown of estrogen. Liver function, bile secretion, bacterial balance and frequency of bowel movements are essential processes for ridding the body of excess estrogen which has been known to increase cancer risks.

A bowel movement after each meal is perfect bowel function. Cleansing your digestive system will clear your complexion and improve your energy levels as you gain a sense of well-being. Improving intestinal wall competency will also aid absorption of nutrients and water, while preventing absorption of unhealthy bacteria and incompletely digested food or toxins.

For optimal bowel health I recommend adding in a probiotic twice daily, ground flaxseeds or a non-psyllium fibre source, magnesium glycinate to bowel tolerance. If you are prone to constipation you can also consider adding in the herb Triphala, an Ayurvedic herbal blend commonly used for supporting intestinal detoxification, occasional constipation and overall colon health.

CLEAR IT OUT

If your urine is bright yellow it's an easy sign that you need to up your water intake.Your kidneys flush waste from the blood and without enough water they can't do their job very well. The human body is also extremely good at preserving water if you don't drink enough (and in turn, your rings may not fit at the end of the day).

Herbal teas that have a blend of goldenrod, dandelion leaf and parsley will help get your bladder going. In turn, some veggies such as celery stalks and cucumbers are great natural diuretics. If you enjoy two cups of water before each meal and snack you will most likely meet your water goal, and you may be surprised to find that you look and feel slimmer when fully hydrated.

Love the skin you're in

You can and should sweat out your toxins regularly. Your skin is a source of toxin elimination, and like your lungs, it can both absorb toxins and release them.

Exercise is a great and easily accessible way to burn calories and excrete toxins, ensuring that you work up a sweat three times a week for 30 minutes. I also recommend the use of an infrared sauna one to three times a week.

Not to be confused with a regular dry sauna, an infrared sauna penetrates more than 1.5 inches into the body. It helps immensely with estrogen detoxification, circulation, fat loss, skin health, athletic performance and improved immune response. While the mechanism is not entirely understood, a 20 to 40 minute session can also boost your mood and calm your nervous system.

While in the sauna I recommend adding a teaspoon of buffered vitamin C and ¼ tsp of Celtic sea salt into a 1L jug of water and drinking regularly to replenish electrolytes and expedite the detoxification process.

If you don't have access to an infrared sauna you can use good old fashioned epsom salt baths. Simply place 1 to 2 cups of epsom salts into a warm bath and let yourself relax for 20 minutes.

Lastly, consider brushing your skin daily. This improves lymphatic drainage, boosts immunity and removes dead skin cells. Look for a natural bristle brush with a long handle and practise brushing your skin (in the direction of your heart) before showering at least once per day.

Physical features, however, are not what I mean when I use the word "beautiful." We are programmed and bombarded with images of what physical "beauty" is. My 6 year old daughter has asked me if she's "pretty" after watching television. Images of this pre-programmed model of beauty surround women at every turn from billboards to television commercials, beauty magazines, and music videos.

They are narrow images; a droplet of water in a vast ocean of beauty. Most women that I know have a laundry list of things that they want to change about themselves; an inner dissatisfaction with some aspect of their appearance.

As I approach my late 30's and have a daughter of my own, I've taken some steps to love myself a bit more; trying on a daily basis to know my worth and to stop being so hard on myself for not fitting the into the program.

This not only feels so much healthier for my mind, body, and spirit, but I want to be a positive model for my daughter.

Self-loathing and constant dissatisfaction is damaging not only to our health (our bodies hear the messages of our mind), but to our relationship to the world around us.

How can we love deeply if we cannot first love ourselves? I've made some small changes in my daily life that have truly helped in my progression of self-love.

Some days, I still agonize over certain physical attributes, I'm human and breaking a habit that it took decades of mental conditioning to build is not easy.

My journey through my yoga practice, lots of meditation and self-observance have taught me how to better focus more on who I am in my own heart and who I want to be in the world, rather than quantifying that through physical attributes.

Who we surround ourselves with is so unbelievably important and a direct reflection of how we feel about ourselves. Surrounding ourselves with people that see our beauty and encourage us to be our best selves is crucial.

When I began really thinking about who elevates me in my life, who is on a similar path, and who is truly compassionate and loving in our shared humanity- I realized who I want my tribe to be.

Anyone that may tear you down in the name of "honesty"; a person that is chronically critical or negative is not your tribe member. Loving yourself often means walking away from relationships that are stagnant or feel toxic.

People that elevate your spirit, are like-minded and encouraging... seek that. Feed and nurture those relationships and watch them flourish. Find your tribe and watch how much more confident you feel.

Think of what your physical body has allowed for today. Simple things are often miracles that we forget to acknowledge. Having broken my back in two places and faced the possibility of paralysis has truly helped me marvel in my blessings. Jogging up steps when I'm in a rush, or ...just because, always stirs gratitude in my heart.

Did you have to walk quickly to catch a train today? Did you meditate and truly experience awareness of your breath? Did you practice yoga and really use your muscles? Did you lift your child? Our bodies are miracles. A beating heart... a brain that controls every movement...

Notice. Be amazed. How can you not love your body?

As human beings, we all experience feelings of fearfulness, inadequacy, jealousy, or insecurity at certain points in our lives. It's important to stop, take a breath, and check in with yourself. In those moments when the heat rises and we struggle, ask yourself, "What is happening right now?" Often, this question reveals so much.

There is no other brain, physical body, or spirit like yours on the planet. You cannot be duplicated.

That is truly amazing. You are unique. You are beautiful. There is no one else like you.

We all have darkness, bad days, and great struggle. Self-love is the first step toward emerging gracefully through all of it. Lack of self-love can lead to depression, cause us to fall short of our potential, and allows for possibly tolerating abusive situations.

Begin to practice taking action on this amazing journey through radical self love and acceptance. Be fearless.

HERBAL CLEANSE

You may have heard of a herbal cleanse before and you might have wondered if it was right for you. Using all natural ingredients to cleanse your body and eliminate toxins can provide you with some amazing health benefits.

What kind of problems can a natural cleanse help you with? For instance, bloating is a common health problem for those who eat too much. Taking digestive pills and even home remedies don't always bring relief.

A herbal cleanse is one way to get your health back on track. Many people swear by its effectiveness and how amazing they feel after they have done one. This type of cleanse is a tool to help detoxify your body from the inside out.

Most people will do a herbal cleanse to bring relief from bloating and gas, along with stomach problems. It can also eliminate toxic wastes from the colon and make you feel great.

Herbal Cleanse Benefits

- Detoxify Colon
- Cleanse Gall Bladder
- Cleanse Liver
- Increase Energy
- Purify The Entire System
- Provide Extreme Antioxidants To The Body
- Help To Lose Weight Naturally

Many who suffer from chronic stomach problems have found that a herbal cleanse can really help them feel better. It can flush all of the toxins out of the stomach and the rest of the body.

This can positively impact your health with little to no side effects. A lot of people have noted that they have increased energy levels after doing a herbal cleanse.

This could be because of the toxins that have been cleansed from the body.

It is a great way to optimize waste elimination and aid in the process of digestion. An all-natural version of a colon cleanse will enhance the overall feeling of good health.

Natural ingredients found in herbal cleanses have also found to be effective at helping with weight loss.

This is primarily because when you use a herbal cleanse you are ridding the body of toxins and built up waste.

This waste has weight, so when you remove it you will automatically lose weight.

The amount of waste that is stuck in everyone varies.

Herbal cleanses are generally safe to use and can be combined with your normal diet.

Many people notice that they have a flatter and more toned body after an herbal cleanse. It can improve your metabolism and overall health.

Getting rid of extra weight and removing harmful toxins from the body are the best benefits in doing a herbal cleanse.

A herbal cleanse can help you with certain digestive issues and other health disorders.

There are reports of people with allergies and hemorrhoids seeing the benefits too. If there is too much waste in the colon it can become impacted and cause serious health issues.

This can not only become painful, but it can also be a breeding ground for infection.

Using a herbal cleanse can have some pretty positive effects on your health. It can put you on the right path to a healthier lifestyle.

If you are dealing with bloating and weight gain, then a herbal cleanse might be perfect for you!

Also, those who have chronic headaches and constipation could benefit from a natural herbal cleanse. It will cleanse the body from the inside out.

It will also rid the body of any extra body fat. A herbal cleanse will help you achieve a happier and healthier quality of life.

Flushing the built of waste that has been trapped in your body is a great way to detox your body to toxins and other harmful substances.

Detox Diet

Do you want to look fresh and ravishing all day long?

Think your skin, hair, and overall health have deteriorated over time?

It's quite possible that there are too many toxins in your system that are causing breakouts, hair loss, indigestion, constipation, and what not!

Eating oily, unhygienic food and following an unhealthy lifestyle are the root causes of it.

And to deal with this problem, you have to be on an easy-to-follow detox diet.

This detox diet plan will help you flush out and nullify the toxins and give you glowing skin and lustrous hair, improve digestion and metabolism, boost cognitive function, and also aid weight loss.

This book will provide you with 2, 7, and 15 days detox diet plans.

The 3-day detox diet plan, 7 -day, and the 15-day detox diet plan will help cleanse your internal system and de-stress your mind.

So, without much ado, let me tell you how you can look and feel 10 years younger.

3-DAY DETOX DIET PLAN

Some people will do a detox diet cleanse to release harmful toxins from their bodies. The bad news is that no diet can really "detox" your body.

The good news, however, is that you already have systems in place to take care of that function. Experts will tell you that your body's tissues and organs are always removing harmful toxins. So there is no need to go on a special diet to cleanse your body.

But a diet can feel like it provides a detoxifying effect. After you complete a 3-day cleanse diet, your body may look and feel different. And your eating habits are "detoxed" as well.

*D*AY *1. T*HE *24-H*OUR *F*AST

Physiological hunger is the type of hunger you experience when your brain, muscles and internal organs are in a low-energy state.

This is the type of hunger that you experience following a demanding workout. It's the type of hunger you experience when you have exerted significant physical or mental energy, and are in need of fuel to replenish your energy needs. Physiological hunger is the signal to intake carbohydrates, fats, and protein in order to meet the energy requirements of repairing and growing tissues.

Emotional hunger is the type of hunger you experience when a situation or thought process dictates your desire to eat. As opposed to physiological hunger, emotional hunger creates a feeling of true hunger even though the biological requirement for fuel is low or nonexistent.

Understanding the difference between the two of these types of hunger can make a huge difference to your overall health. Do you eat when you're only physiologically hungry?

Do you eat when you're emotionally hungry? Do you eat in both situations?

Performing a single intermittent fast can help you determine the difference between the two types of hunger.

No matter how you slice it, intermittent fasting isn't just good for you, it's GREAT for you. In addition to the physical benefits described above, consciously restricting food intake even for a single 24-hour period can be quite challenging, and helps you establish a true independence from food.

There are endless permutations of intermittent fasting regimens, so I'll present only the ones that are achievable and boast significant short term benefits.

There is no sense in doing intermittent fasting if the direct benefit takes months or years to achieve. Lucky for you, performing a single intermittent fast is a fun experience that can make a noticeable and measurable difference in your health.

The only thing that matters when it comes to eating is that you get the right nutrients into your body at the right amount. This means that eating 4 meals a day isn't better than eating 1 or 30. Your body simply needs the nutrients it needs.

So how do you accomplish this 24-hour fast? You need a gameplan.

At 6pm (or 5pm if you want to eat earlier the next day) on the night before you start your plan, you will have your last meal for the next 24 hours. You won't touch food again until 6pm the next day.

DAY 2. VEGETABLES

This day is dedicated to replenishing all of the nutrients and vitamins that you have depriving your body of. To fix this you are going to consume nothing but the vegetables listed above.

If this sounds like a drag then you are in the wrong frame of mind. This is great because you get to be creative and find new ways to prepare these veggies. Not only are you working on creating a happier body, but you are also working on learning new cooking methods.

This might be the best diet plan ever!

You can decide when you want to consume your vegetables. If you wish to break them up into 4-5 meals throughout the day then go for it.

Day 3. Protein

On this day you are going back to the protein that you had on day 1. The goal here is to have two meals with 25g of protein in it.

The exact same rules apply to the protein as they did on day 1 so don't pull out the ribs and slather them with BBQ sauce.

If you are doing 4 meals a day then meals 1 and 3 can have the protein.

It's your call. Just make sure you get the recommended 25g of protein in you. There are a number of different apps that can help you make sure you are getting the protein that you need.

7-Day Detox Diet Plan

The thought of going on a seven-day detox diet can be incredibly daunting. With so many different diets touted online and in books, it's tough to tell which approach is right for you. And as do-it-yourself detox becomes more and more trendy, it's all too easy to lose sight of the purpose of cleansing: focusing on whole, unprocessed foods that nurture your body and lighten your toxic load. A seven-day detox diet can be helpful if you use it as a way to begin a healthy way forward when it comes to your eating. But embarking on one every now and again to "right" eating and drinking "wrongs" is not a healthy approach.

For a smarter approach to a detox diet, forget the latest fads that can lead to unhealthy eating patterns and follow a more sensible plan that encourages you to get back to healthy-eating basics and make a long-lasting impact on your wellbeing.

From the preparation stages to your post-detox diet, we've got you covered on the healthiest and most effective way to cleanse.

PREPARING FOR DETOX DIET

To stave off common detox reactions such as headache and nausea, try phasing out caffeine, sugar, processed foods, and artificial sweeteners in the days leading up to your detox diet. If you're not ready to give up caffeine altogether, switch to lower-caffeine drinks like green tea, white tea, or matcha.

In the preparation stages, you should also aim to plan your meals for the week. With your eating plan carefully mapped out, you'll be less likely to stray from your detox diet. You may also want to take this time to rid your kitchen of any foods or beverages that might tempt you during your cleanse.

- Red meat, chicken, turkey and any meat products like sausages, burgers, and pate
- Milk, cheese, eggs, cream
- Butter and margarine
- Any food that contains wheat including bread, croissants, cereals, cakes, biscuits, pies, pastry, quiche, battered or breadcrumbed foods, etc
- Crisps and savoury snacks including salted nuts
- Chocolate, sweets, jam and sugar
- Processed foods, ready meals, ready-made sauces and takeaways
- Alcohol
- Coffee and tea
- Sauces, pickles, shop bought salad dressing, mayonnaise
- Salt
- Fizzy drinks and squashes, including diet versions

Banana porridge

Porridge made with water and topped with natural yoghurt, banana, raisins and sweetened with honey.

Fruit salad with yoghurt and oats

Fresh fruit salad with natural yoghurt and a sprinkling of oats.

Fruit smoothie made with fresh or frozen fruit.

Fruit smoothie made from fresh fruit, natural yoghurt and honey to sweeten if needed.

Muesli and yoghurt

Homemade muesli made from oats, seeds, nuts and dried fruit served with natural yoghurt.

Fresh fruit and yoghurt

Fresh fruit and a pot of natural yoghurt sweetened with honey.

Vegetable soup and oatcakes

Large bowl of vegetable or lentil soup (either homemade or supermarket 'fresh') with oatcakes.

Tuna and sweetcorn jacket potato and salad

Jacket potato topped with tuna (canned in water) mixed with sweetcorn and natural yoghurt and served with salad.

Mediterranean salad with rice cakes

Rice cakes served with rocket, avocado, tomatoes, fresh basil and black pepper. Plus a handful of unsalted nuts.

Guacamole with crudités

Homemade guacamole made from avocado, lemon juice, fresh chilli, tomatoes and garlic served with vegetable crudités and oatcakes.

Tzatziki with crudités

Homemade tzatziki made from natural yoghurt, garlic, cucumber and lemon juice served with vegetable crudités and oatcakes.

Avocado and prawn salad

Fresh avocado served with prawns, salad, balsamic vinegar and lemon juice.

Jacket potato with grilled cod

Grilled cod fillet served with jacket potatoes and lightly steamed vegetables.

DETOX PLAN SNACKS

Fresh fruit or fresh fruit salad

Natural yoghurt mixed with honey

Plain popcorn

Handful of unsalted nuts or seeds

Chinese vegetable stir fry

Stir fry a selection of vegetables such as bok choi, spring onions, mushrooms, bamboo shoots and beansprouts in a little olive oil with garlic and ginger.

Serve with brown rice.

Baked salmon with jacket potato

Bake a salmon fillet and serve with a jacket potato and steamed vegetables.

Tuna and prawns with noodles

Gently fry a selection of vegetables such as onions, mushrooms, peppers, courgette and leek in a little olive oil.

When lightly browned, add a handful of prawns.

Cook for a few minutes, then add canned tomatoes, tomato puree, black pepper and tuna canned in water.

Bring to the boil and simmer until the sauce thickens. Serve with rice noodles.

Sweet and sour stir fry with rice

Gently fry a selection of chopped vegetables such as onions, peppers, baby sweetcorn and mushrooms.

Add canned pineapple (in fruit juice), canned tomatoes, tomato purée, white wine vinegar and honey.

Bring to the boil and simmer until the sauce has thickened. Serve with brown rice.

Potato and bean casserole

Gently fry a selection of typical casserole vegetables such as onion, carrots and parsnip in a little olive oil with garlic.

When browned, add diced potato and fry for a few minutes.

Add fresh vegetable stock, black pepper and your favourite beans.

Bring to the boil and simmer until the casserole thickens.

BEDTIME:

Have a warm bath, and try and go to bed no later than 10pm if at all possible. If you do suffer with constipation or IBS symptoms, try giving yourself a gentle abdominal massage with warmed "cold pressed" organic sesame oil.

Use large circular clockwise movements over the lower bowel, every evening after your bath. At the start of your 7-day cleanse, make an effort to clear and clean the bedroom and put clean sheets on the bed.

PLANNING YOUR POST-DETOX DIET

As you journey through your detox diet, you'll likely find that simple changes such as drinking more fluids or eating more vegetables can have a profound effect on your daily wellbeing.

In fact, it's thought that the 7-day approach is an ideal way to experiment with a broad variety of new foods, recipes, and lifestyle habits.

To build on that momentum, ease back into a less restrictive diet while adopting new behaviors (such as eating three servings of vegetables at lunch and dinner).

Research indicates that healthy habits can take up to six weeks to become ingrained—and that treating yourself to small rewards can help motivate you to stick with those positive changes.

Don't try to make too many changes all at once.

Research shows that people form healthy habits more easily when attempting to take on simple actions (such as drinking more water) rather than striving to adopt elaborate routines.

15 – Day Detox Diet Plan

For decades health practitioners have been recommending gut cleanses to enhance their patient's health and wellbeing. But this clinical concept has been given a bad rap from cleanses that promise a quick fix but don't give the body the nutrients they need.

My opinion as a qualified, practising nutritionist is that, when done right, a gut cleanse is an essential step towards optimal gut health.

If you're feeling sluggish, have a heavy head, if your digestion is poor or if its time to shed those few extra kilos, it may be time to consider completing a detox.

I love the Totally Natural 15 Day Detox, one of our most popular detox packs. The recommendations below go with the 15 Day Detox.

The gut is the basis of our health – it's the first line of defense against pathogens, it's where we digest and absorb nutrients and where we house our gut microbes, also known as gut bacteria.

Poor gut health is now thought to be strongly linked to a compromised immune system, malnutrition and poor mood regulation, and plays a role in arthritis and obesity.

A gut cleanse is a necessary step in repairing a poor gut.

Why?

A good cleanse will replace foods that aggravate and compromise our gastrointestinal health with gut-friendly foods that do three things – 'heal and seal' the gastrointestinal tract; provide probiotics for healthy gut bacteria; and provide fibre for bowel health. Think of the gut like a car.

A gut cleanse is like a service, and gut-friendly foods and supplements are like premium fuel.

Water with lemon, cooked quinoa, flax oil, nuts or seeds (for protein), and unsweetened dried fruit.

Water with lemon, fruit smoothie or a large bowl of fresh fruit with yogurt, flax or hemp seeds, and spirulina.

Water with lemon, leftover kitchari, sauerkraut.

Cup of hot water and lemon upon rising then juice the following ingredients:

Chunk of cucumber

1 pear

Handful of spinach

Handful of parsley

Juice of ½ a lemon

½tsp grated ginger

Kombucha; leftover baked sweet potato, mashed; mixed salad with grated carrots, sprouts, and lemon miso tahini dressing or flax oil and balsamic vinegar; leftover black bean stew or carrot-ginger soup.

Salad of mixed greens with grated or boiled beets and lemon miso tahini dressing or flax oil and balsamic vinegar; leftover quinoa tossed with any chopped raw vegetables and flax oil and balsamic vinegar; black bean stew.

Herbal tea, kitchari, steamed collards with lemon miso tahini dressing.

Sweat 1 onion, 1 celery stick and 1 carrot. Pour in 300ml vegetable stock, 200g garden peas and a handful of fresh mint. Add 1tbsp low-fat crème fraîche and blitz until smooth.

Steamed Bass with Fennel, Parsley, and Capers

This recipe was adapted from "Clean" and makes two servings, you can share with a friend, keep one portion for the next day, or halve the recipe. If desired, you can serve one cup of steamed brown rice per person on the side

Apple Almond Butter Overnight Oats

I love this breakfast recipe year round and simply change it up depending on what's in season. I keep it simple and use ingredients you most likely already have stocked in your fridge. During the summer, I top it with berries. In the winter, I use coconut milk and citrus, and in the fall, it's all about apples, pears, pomegranates, and persimmons. Plus, it's packed with protein, healthy fats, and fiber to keep you full all morning long.

Yields 2 servings

Ingredients

1 1/2 cups plant-based milk (almond or cashew work well)

1 cup rolled oats, gluten free as needed

1 1/2 Tbsp of chia seeds

2 Tbsp almond butter, plus more for topping

1 dash of cinnamon

1 apple, grated

1 handful of sliced almonds, toasted

Drizzle of raw honey, hemp hearts, and any other superfood topping desired!

Salmon and Cauli Rice Bowl

A nearly foolproof way to cook salmon? Slow roasting. It's delicious on its own, on salads, in bowls, and more. Here, I serve it with cauli rice, veggies, avocado, and a soft-boiled egg for an easy, satisfying dinner.

Yields 2 servings

Ingredients

Salmon

1/2 lb. thick salmon fillet

4–5 sprigs of mixed herbs (I use chives, rosemary, and thyme.)

Lemon zest

Drizzle of olive oil

Kosher salt and freshly ground black pepper, to taste

Cauli rice

1/2 large cauliflower or 1 small cauliflower whole

Olive oil

Pink salt and freshly ground black pepper, to taste

Garnishes

2 handfuls of baby lettuce, arugula, or your favorite greens

1 cup steamed green beans

1/2 cup baby purple potatoes, sliced

1 soft-boiled egg

1/4 cup capers, drained

1 avocado, halved, pitted, and sliced

CFDC Vinaigrette

1/2 small shallot, finely minced

1/4 cup lemon juice (about 2 lemons)

1/2 cup olive oil

Sweet Potato Bowl

This lunch recipe is a take on the one in my cookbook, Good Clean Food. It's super easy to throw a few more seasonal ingredients on the same roasting tray to make for a perfectly balanced bowl. Tip: Double or triple the dressing to use throughout the week, or on the slow-roasted salmon bowl below.

Yields 2–3 servings

Ingredients

Bowl

1 small head of cauliflower or 1/2 of a larger head, cut into small florets

1 sweet potato, cut into 1/2-inch cubes

1 15 oz. can of chickpeas, rinsed and drained

2 Tbsp coconut oil, melted

2 tsp curry powder

3/4 tsp turmeric

1 pinch of red pepper flakes

1 cup mixed quinoa, millet, and buckwheat

1/4 cup sliced almonds, toasted

1/4 cup cilantro, roughly chopped

Juice of 1 lime

Olive oil

Pink salt and freshly ground pepper, to taste

Few handfuls of greens, arugula, chopped spinach, or chopped kale

Clean Food Dirty City Vinaigrette

1/2 small shallot, finely minced

1/4 cup lemon juice (about 2 lemons)

1/2 cup olive oil

2 tsp dijon mustard

Pink salt and freshly ground black pepper, to taste

Detox Smoothie Recipes

A good detox smoothie recipe should include a mix of fresh fruits and vegetables that fight inflammation and toxins while nourishing and rebuilding any damaged tissues or organs. Herbs, spices, nuts, and seeds are also great for keeping you fuller longer as well as for providing necessary omega fatty acids.

Glowing Green Detox Smoothie

1 kiwi

1 banana

¼ cup pineapple

2 celery stalks

2 cups spinach

1 cup water

Green Protein Detox Smoothie

½ cup unsweetened almond milk

1 tablespoon almond butter

1 banana

2 cups mixed greens (I like kale, chard and spinach)

Apple Berry Detox Smoothie

1 cup mixed berries (like raspberries, strawberries, and blueberries)

1 large apple

2 cups spinach

1 cup water (or unsweetened almond milk)

Pineapple Banana Detox Smoothie

1 cup pineapple

1 banana

1 apple

2 cups spinach

1 cup water

Strawberry Banana Detox Smoothie

1 banana

1 cup yogurt (plain)

1 cup strawberries (fresh or frozen)

1 cup Kale (chopped)

1 cup ice

Pineapple Coconut Detox Smoothie

1 banana

1 cup pineapple

1 cup coconut water

2 cups kale (chopped)

Apple Green Detox Smoothie

⅔ cup almond milk (unsweetened)

¾ cup ice

1 ½ cups kale (chopped)

1 stalk celery (chopped)

½ red or green apple (cored and chopped)

1 tbsp ground flax seed

1 teaspoon honey (optional)

Avocado Detox Smoothie:

1 1/2 cups apple juice

2 cups spinach or kale (stemmed and chopped)

1 apple (unpeeled, cored, and chopped)

1/2 avocado (chopped)

Tropical Green Detox Smoothie

1 full cup (70g) kale

¾ cup (110g) frozen mango chunks

¾ cup (110g) frozen pineapple chunks

½ banana, sliced

1¼ cup (300 ml) coconut water

Sweetener, to taste (agave, honey, stevia, maple syrup or dates)

½ teaspoon spirulina powder

Cleanse & Detox Smoothie

1 organic apple

Juice of 1 lemon

1 cup kale

1 stalk or rib of celery

1/3 cup flat leaf parsley or cilantro

1 tablespoon ground flax seeds or chia seeds

1/4 teaspoon ground cinnamon

1 1/4 cups chilled water

Banana & Nuts

1 frozen sliced very ripe banana, previously peeled & sliced

1/4 cup almond milk (or your favorite milk such as skim, 1%, soy, cashew, coconut, etc)

1 and 1/4 cups chopped pineapple

1 peach, peeled and sliced

1/2 cup Greek yogurt (or regular yogurt - plain or flavor of your choice)

1 - 2 cups fresh spinach

Juice + zest of 1 lime, optional

Berries Smoothie

1 1/2 cups Berry Mix (Blueberries, Raspberries, Blackberries)

1/2 cup Coconut Milk

1 cup Purified Water

1/8 cup rolled oats

Ginger Spice Smoothie

1 nub Ginger Root

1 tsp Cinnamon

1 handful Spinach

1 cup Purified Water

Cocoa Bliss Smoothie

1 tbsp Dark Cocoa Powder

1/2 cup Coconut Milk

1/2 cup Strawberries

1 cup Ice (if during warmer months)

Green and Clean Smoothie

1/4 Cucumber

1/2 handful Spinach or Other Leafy Green

1/2 Avocado

1 Celery stalk

2 sprigs Fresh Mint

1 Kiwifruit

1 cup Purified Water

1/2 of apple

Squirt of lemon

Vegan Detox & Fat Burn Smoothie

1/2 cup baby carrots

1 tomato

1 celery

1/2 lemon juice

A handful of coriander leaves

1 teaspoon roasted cumin seed powder

Freshly ground pepper

Fruity Kale Detox Smoothie

4 baby kale leaves

1/2 cup green grapes

1/2 grapefruit

1/2 cup watermelon

A handful of mint leaves

1/2 teaspoon pepper

Spinach Cucumber Cooling Detox Smoothie

1 cup spinach leaves

1/2 cucumber

1/2 lemon

A handful of mint leaves

1/2 teaspoon roasted cumin powder

Coconut Water & Berries Detox Smoothie

1 glass tender coconut water

1/2 cup tender coconut

1 cup strawberries

1 medium sized gooseberry

2 blueberries

Mint leaves

PLANT BASED DIET

A plant-based diet is any diet that focuses around foods derived from plant sources.

This can include fruit, vegetables, grains, pulses, legumes, nuts and meat substitutes such as soy products.

People often have different interpretations of what 'plant-based' eating looks like.

Some people still include small amounts of animal products such as meat and fish, while focusing mainly on vegetarian foods – this is referred to as a semi-vegetarian or flexitarian diet.

Plans that cut out meat but still include fish are referred to as pescatarian diets.

People who don't eat meat or fish but still include dairy and eggs are referred to as vegetarian, while those who cut out any animal derived products, including dairy, eggs, honey and gelatin are referred to as vegan.

People following plant-based diets and consuming a wide variety of fruits, vegetables and pulses are likely to find it easier to meet their five-a-day target.

Due to this, they are also likely to have good intakes of fibre and the vitamins and minerals that are present in fruit and vegetables, including folate, vitamin C and potassium, all of which are important for good health.

However, it is worth noting that 'plant-based' does not automatically mean 'healthy', particularly when it comes to processed and packaged foods.

Technically, products such as refined sugar, white flour and certain vegetable fats can all be labelled 'plant-based' as they are vegetarian, but this does not mean that they should make up the bulk of a healthy diet.

When following a plant-based diet there are some key nutrients that you should focus on.

These include protein, vitamin B12, the vitamins and minerals needed for bone health including calcium and vitamin D as well as the essential omega-3 fatty acids.

Certain nutrients are not found very easily in plant foods, including vitamin D and B12 as well as omega-3 fatty acids.

These may need to be sourced from fortified foods such as fortified plant milks, spreads and cereals.

If you are considering taking a supplement to support your nutritional intake, discuss this with your GP or doctor first.

www.ingramcontent.com/pod-product-compliance
Lightning Source LLC
Chambersburg PA
CBHW031739150726
47989CB00006B/2529